MARIO GUZMAN

The Family Business Exit Plan

How to Pass the Business to the Next Generation Without Losing It

For my beloved wife, Karina, and my wonderful son, Erik. Thank you for your endless love and support.

Contents

Author's Note

———————◆———————

Throughout this book, I share stories of business owners, families, and successors navigating the complexities of family business transitions. Characters such as Robert and Daniel, Carol, Gary, Miguel and Sofia, Jim, Ray and Elena, and David and Marcus are **composite figures;** they are not real individuals. Their names, circumstances, and personal details are fictional.

However, the situations they face, the mistakes they make, and the breakthroughs they experience are drawn directly from real patterns I have observed over my years as a business consultant. Each story is grounded in actual outcomes, research, and the lessons learned from working with family-owned businesses across industries.

I chose to write the book this way intentionally. Following the journeys of specific characters makes complex topics like valuation, succession planning, and family governance more relatable and easier to understand than abstract theory alone. By walking alongside these characters, you will see the principles of *The Five Pillars* come to life in ways that reflect the real challenges and real victories of family business succession.

Any resemblance to actual persons, living or deceased, or actual businesses is purely coincidental.

———————◆———————

Mario A. Guzman
Miami, Florida

Introduction

The Moment of Truth

Seventy percent of family businesses don't survive the transition to the second generation. Of those that do, only thirteen percent make it to the third. (These figures, widely cited across family business research, draw from studies by the Family Business Institute and corroborating data from Harvard Business School and the Conway Center for Family Business.)

Read those numbers again. They mean that the company you spent decades building, the one that paid for your home, put your kids through school, and gave your family its identity, has roughly a seven-in-ten chance of dying the moment you step away from it.

And here's what no one talks about: the businesses that fail rarely fail because of the market, or the competition, or bad luck. They fail because the transition itself was handled incorrectly. The founder waited too long. The successor wasn't ready. The family couldn't separate kitchen-table emotions from boardroom decisions. The estate plan protected wealth on paper but destroyed the operation in practice.

If you're a business owner who built something real, something that employs people, supports families, (Oh! and it carries your name), you already feel the weight of this. You know you need a plan. You may have even started one. But somewhere between the accountant's spreadsheet and your son's reluctance to talk about the future, the whole thing stalled.

This book exists because stalling is how businesses die.

What you're holding is not a theoretical framework. It's a field-tested, step-by-step blueprint for transferring ownership, leadership, and legacy to the next generation, while keeping the business intact, the family relationships whole, and your financial future secure. You will learn how to identify the right successor (even when the answer isn't obvious), structure the deal so it actually works for everyone, navigate the tax and legal landmines that destroy unprepared families, and have the conversations that most families avoid until it's too late.

Every chapter gives you something you can act on immediately. No fluff. No war stories designed to impress you. Just the plan you need, built by someone who has watched families get this right, and watched others lose everything because they didn't.

But before we build the plan, we need to be ruthlessly honest about what destroys them. Because every failed transition that I have seen traces back to the same small set of mistakes. These mistakes are predictable, preventable, and far more common than any business owner wants to believe.

Chapter 1 starts there. And I'll warn you now: you're going to recognize yourself in at least one of them.

CHAPTER ONE

Why Most Family Business Transitions Fail

Robert spent thirty-four years building a plumbing supply company from a single truck and a leased warehouse into a $12 million operation with forty-seven employees. He worked every Saturday for the first decade. He missed school plays. He skipped vacations. And when it was finally time to hand the business to his son Daniel, who had worked there for eight years and was, by all accounts, ready, the whole thing nearly fell apart in six months.

It wasn't the market. It wasn't a bad economy. It wasn't even Daniel.

It was Robert. Who couldn't stop calling the warehouse manager directly. Who kept approving vendor contracts that Daniel thought he'd been given authority over. Who showed up uninvited to a meeting with their biggest client because he "just wanted to say hello."

Within a year, three key employees had quit. Daniel was demoralized. Robert was resentful. And the business, the thing they both loved, was caught in the middle.

Robert didn't fail to plan. He failed to *let go*. Those are two very different problems, and both will destroy a transition.

I've seen versions of this story more times than I can count. And what strikes me every time is this: the business was fine. The successor was capable. The finances were solid. The transition failed anyway, because nobody had dealt with the invisible stuff.

That's what this chapter is about. Not the mechanics of succession, we'll get to those. This is about understanding, honestly and clearly, why so many transitions fail. Because you cannot build a plan that works until you understand what breaks them.

The Three Killers of Family Business Succession

In my experience working with family businesses, the vast majority of troubled transitions share one or more of three core failure patterns. They're not complicated. They're not rare. And almost every owner I've worked with has recognized themselves in at least one of them.

Killer One: Silence. Nobody ever said it out loud.

The founder assumed their eldest child would take over. The eldest assumed the same. The second child thought there'd be a conversation. The son-in-law who'd worked in the business for twelve years assumed his contribution would be recognized. The non-family CFO assumed the family would eventually ask for his input.

Nobody was wrong, exactly. They were all just operating on different assumptions that had never been tested, because nobody had ever sat down and actually talked about it.

This is more common than you think. Most family business owners are deeply uncomfortable mixing the language of business with the language of family. Talking about who gets what, who leads what, and what happens if someone fails feels too cold, too transactional, too much like admitting you're going to die someday. So it doesn't happen. Until it has to. Which is always at the worst possible time.

Every year you delay having the succession conversation, you pay what I call the *Silence Tax*, a compounding cost paid in the form of misaligned expectations, unchallenged assumptions, and decisions that are harder to reverse. The conversation gets more expensive the longer you wait.

Killer Two: Sentimentality. Love is a terrible hiring criterion.

Consider the Delgado family, who ran a successful regional restaurant group, five locations, solid margins, and a brand that people in their city genuinely loved. The patriarch, Miguel, always assumed his daughter Sofia would take over. Sofia worked in the business through college, knew the operation, and loved the brand.

But Sofia was not a leader. She was warm, hardworking, and deeply committed, and completely unable to make hard decisions or hold her managers accountable. Within eighteen months of taking the reins, staff turnover had doubled. Two locations were underperforming. The brand that Miguel spent twenty-two years building was quietly eroding.

Miguel had made the most human mistake possible: he chose the person he wanted to succeed, rather than the person the business needed.

This isn't cruelty. It's clarity. The most loving thing you can do for both your family and your business is to be honest about fit. Sometimes the right successor is a family member. Sometimes it's a hybrid, a family member in partnership with a strong non-family operator. Sometimes the business needs outside leadership for a generation before the next family member is ready. There is no wrong answer. There is only the honest one, and the one you're avoiding.

Killer Three: Procrastination. *"We'll deal with it when the time comes."*

I have heard this sentence, in various forms, from hundreds of business owners. And the time always comes, but rarely in the way they imagined. A health crisis. A key employee who suddenly leaves. A spouse who finally says enough. A competitor who makes an offer. An unexpected tax bill that makes the owner realize they have no idea what their business is actually worth.

These aren't hypotheticals. These are the moments that force succession conversations that should have started years earlier, and now they must happen under pressure, with incomplete information, in the middle of a crisis.

A well-executed succession plan typically takes three to seven years to implement properly. Not because the paperwork is complicated, but because the human side takes time. Developing a successor takes time. Restructuring finances takes time. Building governance takes time. Doing all of that while also running a business takes time. Experts who study family business transitions consistently find that roughly seventy percent fail to survive the transition to the second generation, and nearly ninety percent don't make it to the third. Procrastination is the single largest contributor to those statistics.

The Founder's Trap

Here's the thing nobody tells you when you start a business: the skills that make you great at building it are often the exact skills that make it hard to leave.

You are decisive, so decisions pile up on your desk because nobody else is trusted to make them. You have deep customer relationships, so clients call you directly, even after you've "handed over" account management. You know every corner of the operation, so when something goes sideways, people come to you, not your successor.

This is the Founder's Trap: you built a business that cannot function without you, not because you wanted it that way, but because that's what high performers naturally do when nobody forces them to build differently. The business that was an asset for thirty years becomes a liability the moment you try to step away from it, because its value was never really in the systems, the brand, or the product. It was in *you*.

A business that depends on its owner to function is not a business. It's a job you happen to own. And you can't transfer a job, only a business.

The good news: this is fixable. But it requires deliberate work to document processes, delegate authority, develop leaders, and slowly remove yourself from the critical path, before the exit, not during it.

When Family Dynamics Become Business Liabilities

Every family carries invisible scripts, patterns, loyalties, wounds, and expectations that developed over decades. Usually, they stay in the background. But when ownership, money, and power enter the picture, those scripts get loud.

The older sibling who always felt overlooked. The parent who plays favorites. The in-law who resents being treated as an outsider after fifteen years. The non-participating sibling who contributed nothing but expects an equal share of the exit.

These dynamics don't disappear when people walk into the office. They get reenacted, in compensation disputes, in org chart decisions, in whose calls get returned and whose don't.

I worked with one family where the real succession blocker had nothing to do with business readiness. It was that the founder's two sons hadn't spoken naturally to each other in three years, a fallout from a personal dispute that had never been resolved. One was being set up to lead the business. The other co-owned it. There was no governance structure in place. There were no formalized buyout rights. You can guess how that ended.

The solution isn't to fix every family relationship before you can work on the business. That's a lifetime project. The solution is to build structures - governance, legal agreements, clear roles, defined ownership rights - that allow the business to function professionally even when the family relationships are complicated.

Business structure is not a substitute for family communication. But it is a shock absorber. And in a transition, you need every shock absorber you can get.

What You Can Do Right Now

Understanding why transitions fail is only useful if it moves you to act differently. Here are three concrete things to do before you start the next chapter:

1. **Do the Honest Audit.** Ask yourself this question and actually sit with it: if you were hit by a bus tomorrow, what would happen to the business in thirty days? Ninety days? One year? The answer tells you how founder-dependent you really are, and how urgent the work ahead is.
2. **Name the Assumptions.** Write down, in plain language, what you believe every key person in your family and business expects to happen when you step back. Then write down what you think they actually

know for certain. The gap between those two lists is the Silence Tax you're currently paying.

3. **Identify Your Biggest Threat.** Of the three killers (Silence, Sentimentality, and Procrastination), which one is most alive in your situation right now? Name it. Write it down. You don't have to solve it today. But you cannot solve what you won't name.

What Comes Next

Knowing what breaks transitions is powerful. But it's only half the picture. The other half is knowing exactly what a successful transition looks like, what the plan contains, how it's structured, and what sequence of decisions leads from where you are today to a business that is transferred, protected, and thriving.

Robert, by the way, eventually got it right. It took eighteen months of hard work, some difficult conversations, and one very uncomfortable session with a family business consultant. Daniel is now running the business. Robert is on the advisory board, with a clear, agreed-upon scope for what that means. The warehouse manager came back.

Your plan starts in the next chapter.

Now that you can see the traps, it's time to build the path around them. In **Chapter 2: The Exit Plan Framework → Your Roadmap**, we're going to construct a complete transition blueprint from the ground up. The five pillars, a timeline you can actually use, and a self-assessment that will show you, with brutal honesty, exactly where you stand today and what needs to happen next.

CHAPTER TWO

The Exit Plan Framework - Your Roadmap

Carol knew she wanted to retire at sixty-five. She was fifty-eight when she first said it out loud.

She owned a third-generation printing business, the kind of company that had survived the desktop publishing revolution, the internet, and two recessions through sheer stubbornness and adaptability. Her son Ethan was in the business. Her daughter was not. Her key operations manager, a non-family employee named Theresa, had been there for nineteen years and knew the business almost as well as Carol did.

Carol had seven years. That sounds like plenty. It is not. Not if you spend the first four years telling yourself you'll get to it soon.

When Carol finally sat down to plan, she was three years from her target exit date. And when she mapped out everything that needed to happen, the valuation, the ownership structure, the succession decision between Ethan and Theresa, the buy-sell agreement, the estate plan, the governance documents, the customer transition plan, she went pale. "I thought I was ahead of this," she told me. "I had no idea how much there was to actually *do*."

Most business owners don't lack the intention to plan. They lack a *map*. They don't know what the plan actually contains, so they keep waiting until they feel ready to start something they can't yet see.

This chapter gives you the map. A complete framework for what a successful exit plan contains, how the pieces fit together, and in what order to build them. By the end, you'll have a scorecard that shows you exactly where you are strong and where you are exposed, so you can stop guessing and start moving.

The Five Pillars of a Successful Exit Plan

An exit plan is not a single document. It is not a conversation you have once with your attorney. It is a system, a set of interconnected decisions and structures that, together, move your business safely from your hands to the next generation.

There are five pillars to that system. Every successful transition I have seen, without exception, had all five in place. Every troubled transition was missing at least one.

Pillar One: Valuation. You cannot plan a transfer you haven't measured. Before any succession decision, legal structure, or financial planning can happen, you need to know what your business is actually worth, not what you hope it's worth, not what you paid for it, not what your neighbor sold his for. The real number.

Valuation drives everything downstream: the tax implications of your transfer structure, the fairness of what each family member receives, the viability of an installment sale or management buyout, and whether the business can support your retirement without a third-party sale. Most family business owners avoid formal valuation because they're afraid of what they'll find. Either the number is lower than they expected, threatening their retirement plan, or higher, making the tax implications daunting. Neither is a reason to stay in the dark. Both are reasons to know *sooner*.

Pillar Two: Succession. Who leads next? This is the question that keeps owners up at night, and for good reason. The wrong answer doesn't just create family conflict. It destroys the value you spent decades building.

Succession planning is not a single decision. It is a process: identifying the right person, developing their capability, creating a structured transition of authority, and managing the handoff of relationships with employees, customers, and suppliers, over time. We'll go deep on succession in Chapter 4. For now, know this: the succession decision and the development timeline are the longest lead-time items in your entire exit plan. You cannot rush them. Which means they need to start first.

Pillar Three: Financial Structure. How the business gets transferred is a financial and legal decision with enormous consequences, for your retirement income, your estate, and your tax bill. Gift it outright? Sell it on installment? Use a trust? Set up a Family Limited Partnership? The right structure depends on your family situation, your financial needs, and your tax picture.

This pillar also includes cleaning up the finances, separating personal from business expenses, normalizing owner compensation, and presenting audit-ready books that reflect the true health of the business. A business with messy financials transfers at a significant discount, or doesn't transfer at all.

Pillar Four: Operations. Remember the Founder's Trap from Chapter 1? This is where you fix it. A transferable business has documented processes, a management team that functions without the owner in the room, diversified customer relationships, and clean contracts and intellectual property.

Think of operational readiness as the difference between selling a house that's been staged and cleaned versus one where the owner is still living in it. The asset might be the same, but the buyer's confidence and the price they'll pay are very different.

One area of operational readiness that is increasingly critical and frequently overlooked: your digital and intellectual property assets. Proprietary software, customer databases, trade secrets, brand trademarks, domain names, social media accounts, vendor portal credentials, and any systems built on the founder's personal accounts rather than company accounts, all of these need to be documented, properly owned by the business entity, and transferable. I have seen transitions stall because the company's website was registered under the founder's personal email, or because critical business software was licensed to an individual rather than the corporation. These are not difficult problems to fix, but they are easy problems to miss until they become expensive ones.

Pillar Five: Family Governance. Rules, created before conflict, are wisdom. Rules, created during conflict, are warfare.

Family governance is the set of agreements, structures, and processes that define how the family interacts with the business, who can work there, how decisions get made, how disputes get resolved, and what happens when a family member wants to sell their stake. A family charter. A board of directors or advisory board. A buy-sell agreement. Clear ownership rights. None of these feel urgent when things are going well. All of them become desperately urgent when things go sideways. Build them now.

Your Exit Readiness Scorecard

Before you read another word, score yourself honestly on each of the five pillars. Use a scale of one to ten, where one means "we haven't started" and ten means "this is fully in place and documented." Don't overthink it. Your gut score is usually the right one.

Pillar	What It Covers	Your Score
Valuation	Do you know what your business is worth today, based on a formal or informal assessment?	___ / 10
Succession	Have you identified your successor and begun a structured development plan?	___ / 10
Financial Structure	Are your finances clean, personal and business separated, and transfer structure planned?	___ / 10
Operations	Could the business run for 90 days without you? Are processes documented?	___ / 10
Family Governance	Do you have a family charter, board structure, and buy-sell agreement in place?	___ / 10

If you scored **40–50**, you are genuinely well-prepared, focus on the gaps and execute. **25–39** means you have a foundation but real exposure; prioritize the lowest scores first. **Below 25**, you are at significant risk, but the good news is you now know exactly where to focus.

Working Backwards: The Exit Planning Timeline

Here is the single most useful shift in perspective I can offer you: stop planning forward from today and start planning backwards from your exit date.

Pick a target date, even a rough one. "I want to be out of day-to-day operations by the time I'm sixty-five." "I want the formal ownership transfer complete within five years." It doesn't have to be perfect. It just has to exist. Now work backwards. Here's what a healthy timeline typically looks like.

Five to seven years out: Foundation. Get a formal business valuation. Begin the succession identification and development process. Start separating personal and business finances. Draft or update your buy-sell agreement. Begin documenting key processes and reducing owner dependency. This is the phase where everything feels theoretical, and nothing feels urgent, which is exactly why so many owners skip it and pay for it later.

Three to five years out: Structure. Finalize your transfer structure with legal and tax counsel. Formalize the successor's role and authority with a transition plan. Establish or strengthen board and governance structures. Begin transferring key customer and supplier relationships to the next leader. Update estate plans to reflect the transition structure. This is where the plan stops being a document and starts being a daily reality.

One to three years out: Execution. Execute the formal ownership transfer mechanisms. Complete the leadership handoff, your successor leads, you advise. Wind down personal financial entanglements with the business. Communicate the transition to employees, customers, and key stakeholders. Define your post-exit role, advisory board, consultant, or full exit.

Carol, who came to us with three years left, had to compress the first two phases into eighteen months. It was hard. It was expensive because she needed more professional support to move quickly. And it worked, but only because she stopped waiting and started moving. The earlier you start, the more options you have. Options are the most valuable thing in any exit plan.

The Four Exit Paths, Which One Is Yours?

Not every family business exit looks the same. Before you can build a plan, you need to know which path you're on. There are four, and each requires a different set of decisions, structures, and timelines.

Path One: Internal Family Transfer. The business passes to one or more family members. This is the most emotionally complex path, but when executed well, it's the most rewarding. It preserves the legacy, keeps the brand in the family, and creates a clear continuity story for employees and customers. It requires the most rigorous work on governance, succession development, and financial structure, precisely because the natural tendency is to rely on trust and relationships instead of legal clarity.

Path Two: Management Buyout. A key non-family employee or management team purchases the business, often through an installment sale or seller financing. This is a strong option when there is no ready family successor, but you have a deep, capable team that knows the business. It typically requires the seller to carry significant financing, which means your retirement income is tied to the business's performance for years after you leave. That's not a reason to avoid it. It's a reason to structure it carefully.

Path Three: Third-Party Sale. You sell to a strategic buyer, a competitor or industry player, or a financial buyer like a private equity firm. This path typically generates the highest immediate liquidity, but it ends the family legacy in the business and requires the highest level of operational and financial readiness to maximize value. Many family business owners use this as a last resort. The wisest ones consider it as one legitimate option among four, and let the right answer emerge from clear thinking rather than emotion.

Path Four: Hybrid. Some ownership transfers to the family. Some sells to management. Some may bring in outside capital for a partial liquidity event while the family retains control. Hybrid structures are increasingly common and increasingly sophisticated, and they require the most careful legal and tax planning of any path. There is no universally correct exit path. The right one is the one that matches your financial needs, your family situation, your successor reality, and what you actually want your legacy to be. The worst path is the one you chose by default because you never thought about the alternatives.

What You Can Do Right Now

Three actions that will move you further in a week than most owners move in a year:

1. **Complete the Scorecard.** Go back to the Exit Readiness Scorecard and score yourself honestly. Circle your two lowest scores. Those are your first priorities, not because the others don't matter, but because your weakest pillar will determine the speed of your entire plan.
2. **Set Your Exit Date.** Pick a target year. Write it down. Tell one person. It doesn't have to be precise, and it will almost certainly shift. But a plan without a destination is just a list of good intentions. The date makes it real.
3. **Name Your Path.** Based on what you know today, your family situation, your successor candidates, and your financial needs. Which of the four exit paths is most likely yours? Write it down. Then write one sentence about what would have to be true for that to work.

You have the map. Five pillars. A timeline. A scorecard. Four paths. You know the shape of the terrain ahead. But here's the thing that trips up more owners than anything else at this stage: they start planning the transfer before they know what they're transferring. You cannot structure a fair ownership deal without knowing what the business is worth. You cannot plan your retirement income without knowing what you'll receive. You cannot have an honest conversation with a successor about what they're taking on without showing them the real financial picture. In **Chapter 3: Valuing What You've**

Built, we're going to pull that number into the light, what your business is actually worth, how to find out, and why what most owners discover surprises them. Because you cannot protect what you haven't measured.

CHAPTER THREE

Valuing What You've Built

Gary had been running his HVAC distributorship for twenty-eight years when his accountant, not a business broker, not a valuation expert, just his regular accountant, mentioned offhand that businesses like his were selling for around four times earnings.

Gary did the math in his head. Four times his average net income. He liked the number. He mentioned it to his wife. He started mentally planning the retirement trip to Portugal.

Two years later, when he actually engaged a business appraiser in preparation for transferring the business to his son, the real number came back forty percent lower.

The problem wasn't that Gary's business was bad. The problem was that Gary's reported earnings did not reflect his actual earnings. He ran two personal vehicles through the business. His wife was on the payroll. He expensed family vacations as "client entertainment." His compensation was well above market rate for his actual role. And he had one customer, a regional property management company, that represented thirty-eight percent of his revenue.

None of that is unusual. Almost every family business owner I've worked with does some version of it. But every one of those decisions, perfectly reasonable in isolation, quietly eroded the *transferable* value of his business.

Your tax strategy and your exit strategy are often in direct conflict. The moves that minimize what you pay the IRS today are frequently the same moves that reduce what your business is worth tomorrow.

This chapter is about understanding that tension, and resolving it. We're going to cover how businesses are actually valued, what's suppressing your number right now, and what you can do in the next two to three years to change it.

Why Family Business Valuations Are Different

If you've ever looked up "how to value a business" and come away more confused than when you started, you're not alone. Valuation is part science, part art, and in family businesses, part archaeology, because you have to dig through years of financial decisions made for tax efficiency, family harmony, or pure convenience before you can see the real business underneath.

Here's the core problem: the financial statements of most family businesses do not reflect economic reality. They reflect a series of choices made to minimize taxes and provide for the family, which is completely rational, until you need those statements to tell a coherent story to a buyer, a successor, or an estate attorney.

There are four distortions that come up in almost every family business I've seen, and understanding them is the first step to fixing your number.

Each of these distortions has to be "normalized" before a true valuation is possible. Normalization means restating the financials to reflect what the business would look like under arms-length, market-rate conditions. It's not fraud. It's not creative accounting. It's the standard practice that every serious buyer and appraiser will apply, whether you do it first or not.

Here's why the math matters so much: every dollar of above-market owner compensation that gets added back to earnings in normalization increases your valuation by your multiple. If your industry trades at four times earnings, every $50,000 in normalized earnings adds $200,000 to your business value. That is not a small number.

The Three Valuation Methods

There are three primary approaches to valuing a private business. Most family businesses end up with a blend of two or all three, but understanding each one separately will help you ask better questions and avoid being surprised by what you hear.

Method One: Income-Based Valuation. This is the most common method for operating businesses, and the one most likely to be used in your transition. The core idea is simple: what is this business worth based on the income it generates?

The two most common income-based metrics are EBITDA (Earnings Before Interest, Taxes, Depreciation, and Amortization) and SDE, or Seller's Discretionary Earnings. SDE is more commonly used for smaller businesses, typically under $5 million in revenue, because it adds back the owner's total compensation to show what a new owner-operator could actually pocket. A valuation multiple is then applied. Multiples vary widely by industry, size, growth rate, customer concentration, and dozens of other factors. A $500,000 SDE business might sell for 2.5 times in a commodity industry with high owner dependency, or five times in a growing, systemized business with diversified customers and a strong management team. The multiple is not fixed. It is negotiated and *earned*. Everything you do to reduce owner dependency, clean up finances, and diversify your customer base moves your multiple up.

Method Two: Asset-Based Valuation. This method values the business based on what it owns: equipment, real estate, inventory, receivables, minus liabilities. It's most relevant for asset-heavy businesses: manufacturing, real estate, agriculture, and heavy equipment. For most service or distribution businesses, asset-based valuation sets a floor: the minimum the business is worth, even if it generated no income. It's rarely the primary method, but it matters if you're trying to understand whether the income-based value is supported by underlying assets.

Method Three: Market-Based Valuation. What are comparable businesses selling for? Market-based valuation looks at recent transactions in your industry, ideally, businesses of similar size, geography, and financial profile, and uses those multiples as a benchmark. The challenge with private businesses is that comparable transaction data is genuinely hard to find. Your M&A advisor or business broker will have access to proprietary databases. Your accountant probably won't. This is one of the many reasons that getting a formal valuation from someone who works in transactions, not just in tax preparation, is worth the cost.

In practice, income-based is usually primary, asset-based sets the floor, and market-based provides the sanity check. A good appraiser will use all three and weight them appropriately for your specific business. If someone gives you a valuation number without explaining their methodology, ask them to explain it. If they can't, find someone who can.

A Word on Tax Structure, Because It Changes the Math

Valuation tells you what your business is worth. Tax structure determines how much of that value you actually keep. The two are in constant tension, and the decisions you make here can swing the net proceeds of your transition by hundreds of thousands of dollars. This is not a do-it-yourself area, you need a tax attorney and a CPA who specializes in business transitions, but you should understand the landscape well enough to ask the right questions.

The most common transfer structures fall into a handful of categories. An installment sale lets you sell the business to your successor over time, spreading the capital gains tax across multiple years and providing you with a steady income stream, but it ties your retirement to the business's future performance. Gifting, whether outright or through a trust, can leverage the annual gift tax exclusion and the lifetime estate and gift tax exemption to transfer significant value tax-free, but it requires careful planning and IRS-defensible valuations. A Grantor Retained Annuity Trust (GRAT) allows you to transfer appreciating assets to the next generation while retaining an annuity stream, potentially reducing or eliminating gift tax on the transferred value. An Intentionally Defective Grantor Trust (IDGT) lets you sell the business to a trust for a promissory note, freezing the value for estate tax purposes while the trust's future growth passes to your heirs tax-free. And if your business is a qualified small business under Section 1202 of the Internal Revenue Code, a portion of the gain on sale, potentially up to ten million dollars, may be entirely excluded from federal capital gains tax.

Each of these structures carries trade-offs in complexity, cost, risk, and control. The right choice depends on your family situation, your financial needs, the size and structure of your business, and the current tax code, which changes more often than most owners realize. The point here is not to choose a structure from a book. It is to walk into your first meeting with a tax advisor knowing enough to have an informed conversation, and to start that conversation at least three years before you plan to transfer. Tax planning done at the last minute is not planning. It is damage control.

Protecting and Growing Your Value Before Exit

Here is the part most valuation conversations skip, and it is arguably the most important part for anyone who has more than two years before their intended exit. You don't just measure value. You *build* it.

The two to three years before a transition are the highest-leverage period in your entire ownership tenure when it comes to value creation. Small, deliberate changes to how the business operates and how it looks on paper can produce disproportionate returns at exit.

1. **Reduce owner dependency.** Document your key processes. Build a management team that can make decisions without you. Every reduction in owner dependency increases your multiple, because it reduces the buyer's or successor's perceived risk.
2. **Fix customer concentration.** If any single customer represents more than twenty percent of revenue, that is a known discount factor in every valuation. You don't have to lose the customer, you need to grow the rest of your base, so no single relationship dominates the picture.
3. **Clean up the financials.** Start now. Begin separating personal expenses, normalizing your compensation, and documenting the add-

backs. Three years of clean financials tell a much more compelling story than one year of clean financials with a footnote explaining the previous two.

4. **Lock in your key people.** Buyers and successors discount heavily for key-person risk. Employment agreements, retention bonuses, and non-solicitation agreements for your top two or three people protect value in ways that nothing else can replicate.

5. **Tighten your contracts.** Customer contracts with renewal terms, supplier agreements that transfer to a new owner, and clear IP ownership are not administrative details. They are value-building assets that sophisticated buyers look for specifically.

Gary, our HVAC owner from the opening, spent eighteen months doing exactly this work before his second appraisal. He restructured his compensation to the market rate. He moved his personal vehicles off the books. He landed two new commercial accounts that reduced his largest customer from thirty-eight percent to twenty-two percent of revenue. He promoted his operations manager and gave her real authority. His second valuation came in thirty-one percent higher than the first. Same business. Better story.

Let me put the math of timing in concrete terms. If your business currently generates $600,000 in normalized earnings and trades at a four-times multiple, your value is $2.4 million. If you spend eighteen months reducing risk and improving operations such that your multiple increases to five times, same earnings, your value becomes $3 million. That $600,000 difference cost you eighteen months of deliberate work. Almost nothing else in business offers that return.

Getting Your Number: A Practical Guide

So how do you actually get a valuation? There are several options, and the right one depends on where you are in your timeline and what you need the number for.

Option One: Informal Estimate. Talk to a business broker or M&A

advisor in your industry. Most will give you a rough range in an initial conversation at no cost, they're hoping to earn your business later. This is useful for a directional sense of where you stand, but not reliable enough for legal documents, estate planning, or ownership transfers.

Option Two: Broker Opinion of Value. A step up from an informal chat, typically running $1,500 to $5,000. A business broker prepares a written opinion of value based on your financial statements and market comparables. More rigorous than an estimate, but still not a certified appraisal. Good for internal planning and initial family conversations.

Option Three: Certified Business Appraisal. Performed by a Certified Valuation Analyst or an Accredited Business Valuation professional, typically costing $5,000 to $20,000 or more. This is what you need for estate planning, legal ownership transfers, buy-sell agreement triggers, and any transaction where the number will be challenged or scrutinized. It costs more. It is worth it.

At a minimum, you need a certified appraisal before any legal ownership transfer, whether that's a gift to a family member, an installment sale, or a trust structure. The IRS scrutinizes family business transfers closely. A defensible, certified valuation is not optional; it is protection.

What You Can Do Right Now

Three moves that will change what your business is worth at exit:

1. **Run Your Own Normalization.** Pull your last three years of tax returns and financial statements. For each year, identify every personal or above-market expense running through the business. Total those add-backs and apply your industry multiple. That gap between your reported earnings and your normalized earnings, multiplied by your multiple, is the hidden value sitting in your books right now, and the first place to look for easy gains.

2. **Identify Your Top Three Value Leaks.** From the five value builders listed above, owner dependency, customer concentration, financial

clarity, key-person risk, contract tightness, which two or three are currently working against you? Write them down. Assign a timeline to each. Value doesn't improve by itself.

3. **Book the Conversation.** Call one business broker or M&A advisor in your industry this week and ask for an initial conversation about what businesses like yours are selling for. You don't have to be ready to sell. You just need to know what the market sees when it looks at a company like yours. That information will change how you run the next three years.

You now know what your business is worth, or you know exactly how to find out, and what to do to change the number before you get there. But valuation answers the question of *what* you're transferring. It doesn't answer the hardest question in any family business succession: *who do you transfer it to?* In **Chapter 4: Choosing and Preparing Your Successor**, we're going to work through how to identify the right person, what to do when the obvious choice isn't the right one, and how to develop a leader who can actually carry what you've built. Because getting the valuation right means nothing if the wrong person is sitting in your chair.

CHAPTER FOUR

Choosing and Preparing Your Successor

Here's the sentence that keeps founders up at 2 a.m., staring at the ceiling: *"Who the hell is going to run this thing when I'm gone?"*

It's a fair question. And if you're asking it, congratulations, you're already ahead of the roughly seventy percent of business owners who never ask it at all and end up scrambling when life forces the issue. A health scare. A burnout. A once-in-a-lifetime opportunity that requires your full attention somewhere else. Succession isn't something that happens to other people. It's coming for you, one way or another. The only variable is whether you'll be ready.

This chapter is about making sure you are.

We're going to walk through how to identify the right person, how to test them before the stakes are sky-high, and how to prepare them so thoroughly that the transition feels less like an earthquake and more like a shift change. But first, let's kill the myth that's probably already forming in your head.

The Clone Trap

Your successor is not a younger version of you. I need you to really hear that, because it's the single most common mistake in succession planning, and it torpedoes more transitions than any other factor.

When Sara Blakely brought in Blackstone as a majority partner for Spanx, the leadership question became immediate: who would run the next chapter? Blakely didn't look for another scrappy inventor who'd cut the feet off her pantyhose in a moment of frustration. She and her partners looked for what the *company needed next,* which was operational excellence, global scaling expertise, and the discipline to build infrastructure around a brand that had grown on charisma and instinct. The company didn't need another Sara. It needed what Sara couldn't be.

Think about it this way: you built this business with a specific set of strengths. Maybe you're a visionary. Maybe you're the closer who can sell ice to a penguin. Maybe you're the technical genius who built the product in your garage. Whatever your superpower is, your successor's job isn't to replicate it. Their job is to take what you've built and carry it somewhere you couldn't carry it alone.

So step one is to stop looking in the mirror and start looking at the map. Where does this business need to go? What skills does that destination require? Your successor should be chosen based on the future, not the past.

The Three Places to Look

Your successor is almost certainly in one of three places: **inside your organization, inside your industry**, or **inside your family**. Each option carries its own gravity, and none of them is automatically right or wrong. Let's break them down.

Internal candidates know your culture, your clients, and your rhythms. They've already proven they can survive in your ecosystem. The risk? They may be so embedded in "how things are done" that they can't see what needs to change. When Tim Cook took over Apple from Steve Jobs, he'd been inside the company for over a decade. He knew the machinery cold. But notice what happened: he didn't try to be another product-launch showman. He leaned into operations, supply chain, and services, his strengths, not Steve's. That's a masterclass in internal succession done right.

External candidates bring fresh perspectives and skills your team may lack. They can challenge sacred cows your insiders wouldn't dare touch. The risk? Culture shock, in both directions. They don't know the unwritten rules, and your team doesn't know them. There's a reason studies show external CEO hires get fired at nearly twice the rate of internal promotions. If you go external, budget at least eighteen months for integration, real integration, not just a desk and a laptop.

Family successors carry the emotional weight of legacy, which is both their greatest asset and their most dangerous liability. Your daughter might be brilliant, but if the team sees her as "the boss's kid," she'll spend her first two years earning credibility she should already have. The most successful family transitions I've seen follow a rule I call the *Boomerang Principle*: the successor leaves the family business for at least three to five years, builds a career somewhere else where the last name doesn't matter, and comes back with battle scars and credentials that belong entirely to them. It's a game-changer.

The Five Traits That Actually Matter

I've watched dozens of successions unfold over the years, some graceful, some catastrophic, and the successful ones share a pattern. The people who thrive in the successor's seat tend to have five traits that matter far more than a resume or an MBA.

Judgment under ambiguity. Running a business means making decisions with incomplete information every single day. Your successor needs to be someone who doesn't freeze when the data is inconclusive. Watch how they behave when a client situation goes sideways with no playbook. That tells you everything.

The ability to earn trust without authority. Before they have the title, can they get people to follow them anyway? This is non-negotiable. If they need the org chart to get things done, they're a manager, not a leader.

Emotional resilience. The top job is lonely. Full stop. There will be weeks when the board is unhappy, a key client is threatening to leave, and two senior people are in a turf war. Your successor needs to absorb that pressure without cracking or, worse, passing it downhill as toxicity.

Strategic restlessness. They should never be fully satisfied. Not in an anxious, neurotic way, in a "what's next, what's better, what are we missing" way. Contentment is fine for a lot of roles. It's death for a leader.

Self-awareness. They have to know what they don't know. The successors who fail fastest are the ones who walk in convinced they already have all the answers. The ones who last are the ones who spend their first hundred days asking questions they're not embarrassed to ask.

The Proving Ground: Test Before You Trust

Here's where most succession plans go from theoretical to practical, and it's where most of them fall apart. You've identified your candidate. Great. Now prove it.

Don't hand them the keys to the whole car. Hand them the keys to a *room*. Then see what happens.

The best method I've seen is what I call the Concentric Circles Approach. You start your successor with a contained project that has real stakes, not a make-work assignment, but something with genuine consequences for the business. Maybe it's launching a new product line. Maybe it's turning around an underperforming division. Maybe it's negotiating a partnership that's been stalled for months.

Then you watch. Not hovering, watching. There's a difference. You're looking for how they build their team, how they communicate up and down, how they handle the inevitable setback, and, this is the one people forget, how they handle a win. Do they take credit or share it? Do they celebrate and move on, or do they immediately start mining the success for lessons? Both matter.

If they pass that test, widen the circle. Give them cross-functional responsibility. Let them sit in on board conversations. Have them handle a client relationship you'd normally manage yourself. Each circle gets bigger, the stakes get higher, and the safety net gets thinner. By the time they're ready for the top job, they've already been doing seventy percent of it.

Howard Schultz used a version of this approach at Starbucks when preparing leadership transitions. He didn't just pick someone and announce it. He put potential successors through increasingly complex operational challenges, international expansion, technology overhauls, brand repositioning, and watched how they navigated each one. By the time a successor stepped into the role, the organization had already seen them *lead*. The announcement was a formality, not a surprise. (Schultz's own relationship with succession was more complicated, he stepped down, came back, stepped down, and came back again. Even deliberate succession planning can be messy. But the underlying method was sound, and it's the method that matters here.)

The Knowledge Transfer Nobody Talks About

Here's the uncomfortable truth about your business: half of what makes it work lives inside your head and has never been written down. The vendor who gives you a better rate because you helped his son get an internship twelve years ago. The client who seems difficult but will move mountains for you if you remember to ask about her garden. The employee who's a quiet genius but will shut down completely if they feel micromanaged.

This is institutional knowledge, and it's worth more than your P&L statement. If you don't transfer it deliberately, it walks out the door with you, and your successor spends two years learning things the hard way that you could have taught them in an afternoon.

Here's your action plan for knowledge transfer, and I'm serious, start this tomorrow:

1. **Map your relationships.** Every key client, vendor, partner, and stakeholder, write down not just who they are but *how* the relationship works. What do they value? What offends them? What's the history? Then start introducing your successor into these relationships gradually, as a peer, not a subordinate.

2. **Document your decision-making.** For one month, keep a simple log. Every significant decision you make, write down what it was,

what information you used, who you consulted, and why you went the direction you did. This isn't for posterity, it's so your successor can see *how you think*, not just what you decide.

3. **Create a "Where the Bodies Are Buried" file.** Every business has them. The contract clause that could bite you in 2027. The regulatory filing that's due every March and will cost you a fortune if you miss it. The informal agreement with your landlord that isn't in the lease. Write it all down. Your successor will thank you, or more accurately, they'll never know just how much pain you saved them, which is exactly the point.

4. **Schedule shadow days.** Once a week, have your successor shadow you through your actual day. Not a curated, best-behavior version, your real day, including the boring parts, the frustrating calls, and the awkward conversations. They need to see the job as it actually is, not as it looks from the outside.

5. **Have the hard conversations early.** Tell them where the business is weak. Tell them what keeps you up at night. Tell them about the competitor that scares you, the market shift you're not ready for, the team member you should have let go two years ago but didn't. Radical honesty now prevents catastrophic surprises later.

The Hardest Part: Letting Go

I need to be direct with you about something. The biggest obstacle to a successful succession isn't finding the right person or teaching them what they need to know. It's you. It's your willingness to actually step back.

I've seen founders do everything right, identify a brilliant successor, prepare them meticulously, set a clear timeline, and then sabotage the entire thing by refusing to let go. They hover. They second-guess. They take back decisions. They tell the team, "I'm still here if you need me," which the team correctly interprets as, "Don't listen to the new person."

Your successor will make mistakes. They will do things differently than you would. Some of those differences will be worse, and some, brace yourself, will be better. Both outcomes require you to be quiet and let the process work.

Set a clean transition date. When that date arrives, *leave*. Not to an office down the hall where everyone can see you. Not to a "consultant" role where you're still in every meeting. Leave. Go start something new. Go travel. Go learn to cook. Whatever it is, give your successor the one thing they need more than your advice: the space to become the leader they're going to be.

You built something remarkable. Now let it outlive you.

Getting the right person in the chair is half the equation. But here's the part nobody warns you about: the moment you start talking about *who* takes over, money gets tangled up with love, loyalty gets confused with compensation, and family dinners start feeling like board meetings. That collision between blood and business has destroyed more companies, and more relationships than any bad successor ever could. In **Chapter 5: Separating Family from Finance**, we'll build the wall between the two, so you can protect both the business and the people you love without forcing one to sacrifice for the other.

CHAPTER FIVE

Separating Family from Finance

Let me tell you about two brothers, I'll call David and Marcus. They built a commercial landscaping company together over fifteen years, started with a single truck and a borrowed mower, grew it into a multi-million-dollar operation with sixty employees and contracts across three counties. They were inseparable. Sunday dinners, family vacations, godfathers to each other's kids. The works.

Then came the buyout conversation.

David wanted to retire. Marcus wanted to keep growing. They'd never formalized their partnership agreement beyond a handshake and a two-page document their uncle's lawyer had drawn up in 2009. There was no valuation methodology. No buy-sell agreement. No clarity on who owned what percentage of the equipment, versus the client list, versus the brand. Within six months, they were in litigation. Within a year, they weren't speaking. Their mother had to choose which son to invite to Thanksgiving.

Fifteen years of brotherhood, destroyed in a single financial conversation they'd been avoiding since day one.

I'm telling you this story not to scare you, okay, maybe a little to scare you, but because it illustrates the most predictable disaster in family business, and it's *entirely* preventable. The wall between family and finance doesn't build itself. You have to pour the foundation, lay every brick, and maintain it with the kind of discipline most families reserve for arguments about the thermostat.

This chapter is your blueprint.

Why Money Makes Family Weird

Before we get to the tactical stuff, we need to talk about why this is so hard in the first place. Because it's not a business problem. It's a psychology problem dressed in a business suit.

In a normal employer-employee relationship, the rules are clear. Someone does work, they get paid, and if the arrangement stops working, both sides can walk away with minimal emotional damage. But in a family business, every financial decision carries a second, invisible weight: *What does this say about how much you love me?*

When you pay your sister less than market rate, she doesn't just feel underpaid. She feels undervalued by someone who changed her diapers. When you give your son a smaller equity stake than your daughter, he doesn't see a business decision. He sees a ranking of which child matters more. When you borrow money from your parents to fund the business and the business struggles, you're not just defaulting on a loan. You're failing the people who raised you.

This is the fundamental tension: families operate on unconditional loyalty, but businesses operate on conditional performance. When you try to run both systems on the same operating platform, one of them breaks. Usually both.

The solution isn't to stop caring about family. It's to build structures so clear and so fair that love never has to compete with money in the same conversation.

The Four Walls You Need to Build

Think of the boundary between family and finance as a house with four load-bearing walls. Remove any one of them, and the whole thing eventually collapses.

Wall One: Separate Roles from Relationships. At the dinner table, she's your mother. In the boardroom, she's the CFO. These are not the same person, and they cannot be treated interchangeably. The most functional family businesses I've encountered create what amounts to a psychological airlock, a deliberate, almost ritualistic shift that happens when they cross from family mode into business mode. One family I worked with literally had a rule: no business talk in any room with a dining table, and no family talk in any room with a whiteboard. It sounds almost silly. It worked beautifully.

The Murdoch family empire offers a cautionary tale of what happens when this wall doesn't exist. The intertwining of family hierarchy with corporate governance at News Corp created decades of succession drama, sibling rivalry played out in boardrooms, and legal battles that became international news. When your family dynamics *are* your corporate strategy, everybody loses.

Wall Two: Market-Rate Everything. This is the one that makes people uncomfortable, and I don't care. Every family member in the business should be compensated at fair market rate for the role they actually perform, not the role you wish they performed, not the role they'd have in a bigger company, and definitely not a rate inflated by guilt or deflated by "we're family."

If your nephew is the warehouse manager, look up what warehouse managers make in your market and pay him that. If your daughter is the VP of Sales, benchmark her compensation against that of other VPs of Sales professionals with similar experience. No more, no less. *More* breeds resentment among non-family employees. *Less* breeds resentment within the family. Market rate is the Switzerland of compensation: nobody's thrilled, but nobody can reasonably argue it's unfair.

Wall Three: Governance That Doesn't Require a Referee. You need a formal governance structure, and "formal" doesn't mean expensive or complicated. It means written down, agreed upon, and followed even when it's inconvenient. At a minimum, you need three documents, and if you don't have them, stop reading this chapter and call a lawyer tomorrow morning.

1. **An operating agreement or shareholder agreement** that spells out ownership percentages, voting rights, decision-making authority, and what happens when owners disagree. Not a two-page handshake document, a real agreement reviewed by attorneys who specialize in family business, not your buddy from law school who mostly does real estate closings.

2. **A buy-sell agreement** that defines exactly what triggers a buyout (death, disability, divorce, departure, disagreement), how the business will be valued when that trigger is pulled, and how the buyout will be funded. This is the document David and Marcus didn't have. It's the document that would have saved their relationship.

3. **A family employment policy** that establishes the rules for how family members enter the business, what qualifications they need, how they'll be evaluated, and under what circumstances they can be let go. Yes, fired. If Cousin Eddie can't be fired, he can't truly be employed, he's just on the family payroll, and everyone in the building knows it.

Wall Four: An Outside Voice in the Room. Every family business needs at least one person in a position of authority who doesn't share the last name. An independent board member, an advisory board, a fractional COO, someone who can say the things no one in the family is willing to say, and who has no stake in the family's emotional dynamics.

This person is your circuit breaker. When Dad insists on promoting his youngest son even though the kid has been with the company for eight months and still can't read a balance sheet, the outside voice is the one who can say, "This isn't ready yet," without causing a nuclear Thanksgiving. When two siblings are locked in a strategic disagreement, and neither will budge because neither wants to "lose" to the other, the outside voice offers a tiebreaker that doesn't feel like a family betrayal.

Find this person. Pay them well. Listen to them even when it hurts.

Especially when it hurts.

The Conversations You're Avoiding

Let's get specific. There are five conversations that every family business needs to have, that almost no family business wants to have, and that will poison everything if they keep getting postponed. I'm going to name them, and I want you to notice which ones make your stomach clench. Those are the ones you need to have first.

The "What's it worth?" conversation. Get a professional, third-party valuation. Not a number you and your brother agreed on over beers. Not what your accountant thinks "sounds about right." A formal valuation from someone accredited, using accepted methodologies, updated at least every two to three years. This number will be the foundation for everything, buyouts, estate planning, equity distribution, even compensation benchmarking. Without it, you're building on sand.

The "What if you get divorced?" conversation. Nobody wants to think about this, which is exactly why you have to. If your brother's marriage falls apart, does his ex-wife now own twenty-five percent of your business? Without the right legal protections, prenuptial agreements, trust structures, properly drafted buy-sell provisions, the answer might be yes. I've watched family businesses get torn apart not by the family members who built them, but by the spouses who left them.

The "What about the family members who don't work here?" conversation. Your eldest daughter runs the business. Your younger son is a teacher. Dad's will splits everything fifty-fifty. Sounds fair, right? It's a ticking time bomb. Your daughter now has a co-owner who doesn't understand the business, doesn't contribute to the business, but wants dividends from the business. Meanwhile, your daughter has been reinvesting profits for growth. Equal isn't always equitable. Smart families separate ownership of business assets from ownership of other assets, give the business to the child who runs it, and equalize with life insurance, real estate, or investment accounts for the others.

The **"What do we do about underperformers?"** conversation. If a non-family employee consistently missed targets, showed up late, and undermined team morale, you'd fire them. When it's your brother-in-law, you make excuses, shuffle responsibilities, and create a fake title that keeps him out of the way but on the payroll. Stop it. It's corrosive. Every non-family employee in your company is watching, and they're drawing conclusions about whether performance actually matters here or whether blood is the only currency that counts.

The **"What happens when I die?"** conversation. Not fun. Very necessary. Who takes over? Is the business a going concern or a liquidation event? Is there enough life insurance to fund a buyout without bankrupting the surviving family members? Do your heirs even *want* the business, or will they sell it to the first buyer who waves a check? You need to know these answers while you're still alive and lucid enough to do something about them.

Making It Work in Practice

Theory is wonderful. Let's talk about Monday morning.

Start by scheduling what I call a **Family Business Summit**, one day, off-site, no spouses, no kids, no phones. Bring every family member who has a stake in the business, whether they work there or not. Hire a facilitator. Not Uncle Larry, who's "good with people." A professional facilitator, preferably one experienced with family businesses. This person's job is to create a space where honest conversation is possible, and nobody gets to pull rank.

At this summit, you're going to accomplish three things. First, you're going to create a shared vision, not your vision imposed on the family, but a genuinely collaborative picture of where this business should go and what role the family should play in getting it there. Second, you're going to identify the structural gaps: which of the four walls are missing or crumbling? Third, you're going to assign accountability. Who is responsible for getting the buy-sell agreement drafted? Who is going to commission the valuation? Who is going to research independent board members? Each action item gets a name and a deadline, written down where everyone can see it.

Then, and this is the part people skip, you do it *again*. Every year. The family summit isn't a one-time event; it's an annual ritual. Businesses change. Families change. The structures you build today will need updating as children grow up, marriages happen, markets shift, and new opportunities emerge. The families who treat governance as a living, breathing system are the ones who make it to the third generation. The ones who treat it as a box they checked once are the ones whose lawyers make a lot of money five years later.

Love Is Not a Business Plan

I want to end this chapter where I started, with David and Marcus. Their story didn't have to end the way it did. If they had separated family from finance early, if they had built the walls, had the uncomfortable conversations, and committed to structure over sentiment, they'd probably still be partners. They'd definitely still be brothers.

The love in your family is real, and it matters more than the business ever will. But love is not a governance framework. Love doesn't adjudicate disputes. Love doesn't establish fair valuation methodologies. Love is what makes you want to get this right, structure is what actually gets it done.

Build the walls. Have the conversations. Protect the business so you can protect the family, not the other way around.

You've drawn the line between family and finance. You know the conversations you need to have and the documents you need to sign. But knowing you need structure and actually *building* it are two very different things. Who sits on the board? Who gets a vote, and on what? How do you create decision-making systems that survive the inevitable moment when two people you love disagree about the future of the company? In **Chapter 6: Building the Governance Structure**, we'll turn these principles into plumbing, the councils, boards, and decision frameworks that keep everything flowing long after you've stepped away.

CHAPTER SIX

Building the Governance Structure

I once sat in a meeting where a family business owner, a woman who had built a $40 million manufacturing company from scratch, turned to her three adult children, all of whom held senior positions, and said: "We need to vote on the expansion." Her eldest son asked the obvious question: "How do we vote? Do we each get one vote? Do you get two? Does ownership percentage count? What happens if it's a tie?"

She stared at him. Then she stared at the table. Then she said, "I don't know. We've never actually voted on anything."

Twenty-three years in business. Tens of millions in revenue. And nobody had ever bothered to establish how decisions actually get made when the people in the room disagree.

That's the governance gap, and it's hiding in almost every family business I've ever encountered. When things are going well, you don't need governance, consensus happens naturally, and the founder's instinct fills in the blanks. But "when things are going well" is not a strategy. It's a weather report. And the storm always comes.

In Chapter 5, we talked about separating family from finance. Governance is how you make that separation structural, how you move from good intentions to enforceable architecture. Think of it this way: if separating family from finance is the philosophy, governance is the plumbing. Nobody wants to think about plumbing until the basement floods.

Let's build your plumbing before the water rises.

What Governance Actually Means (And What It Doesn't)

When most people hear "governance," they picture a Fortune 500 boardroom: polished mahogany, Robert's Rules of Order, a chairman banging a gavel. That image is both intimidating and irrelevant to ninety-nine percent of family businesses. Let's throw it out.

Governance, stripped to its bones, answers three questions: **Who decides what? How do we decide it?** And **what happens when we disagree?**

That's it. Everything else, the committees, the charters, the formal meeting minutes, is scaffolding around those three questions. Some of that scaffolding is useful, and we'll get to it. But if you walk away from this chapter with nothing but clear, written answers to those three questions, you'll be ahead of most family businesses on the planet.

Here's what governance is not: it's not a power grab. It's not a way to strip the founder of authority or sideline family members who've earned their seat. It's the opposite. Good governance protects everyone's voice by ensuring no one's voice can drown out the rest. It's the difference between a conversation and a shouting match.

The Three Rings: Family, Board, Management

The most useful mental model I've seen for family business governance comes from a concept developed at Harvard Business School: the Three-Circle Model. Picture three overlapping rings, **Family**, **Ownership**, and **Management**. Every person connected to your business sits in one or more of these rings, and where they sit determines what kind of governance applies to them.

Your cousin, who owns ten percent of the company but works as a dentist? She's in the Family and Ownership rings, but not Management. She has a right to financial transparency and dividend discussions, but she shouldn't be weighing in on whether you switch inventory software. Your non-family COO? He's in the Management ring only. He needs operational authority and clear performance metrics, but he doesn't get a vote on whether the business stays in the family or gets sold.

The mistake most family businesses make is treating all three rings as one ring. Everybody gets a say in everything, which means nobody has clear authority over anything. The result is decision paralysis, end-runs around formal channels ("I'll just call Mom"), and festering resentment from non-family employees who watch real decisions get made at Sunday dinner instead of Monday's leadership meeting.

Each ring needs its own governance structure. Let me walk you through what that looks like in practice.

Ring One: The Family Council

The family council is where family-level decisions live. Not business strategy, family strategy. This is the group that discusses whether the next generation should be encouraged to join the business, how the family's values should influence company culture, what the family's philanthropic priorities are, and how to handle the emotional dynamics that inevitably surface when family and money coexist.

If you're a smaller family business, say, two to five family members involved, your family council might just be a quarterly dinner with an agenda. That's fine. The point isn't to create bureaucracy. The point is to create a dedicated space where family concerns get aired before they metastasize into business problems.

Here's what belongs on a family council agenda, and what doesn't.

Belongs: Family employment policies, dividend philosophy, education and development for next-generation members, conflict resolution between family members, family values and mission, and the emotional experience of working together. These are topics that a traditional board of directors would handle badly because they require vulnerability, not votes.

Doesn't belong: Hiring decisions for non-family roles, operational budgets, marketing strategy, vendor selection, or any other decision that should be made on business merit rather than family sentiment. The moment the family council starts functioning as a shadow board, you've collapsed the rings back into one, and you're right back where you started.

The Cargill-MacMillan family, which has controlled Cargill, the largest private company in the United States, across six generations, offers a remarkable example of family council discipline. They established formal family governance structures decades ago, including clear rules about family participation in the business, educational requirements for family members seeking leadership roles, and a family council that is explicitly separate from the corporate board. The result? A family of over a hundred members that still operates as a relatively cohesive ownership group, which in the world of multi-generational family business is practically a miracle.

Ring Two: The Board (And Why You Need One Even If You Think You Don't)

I can already hear the objection: "I'm a $5 million company. I don't need a board of directors." You're right, you probably don't need a *statutory* board with fiduciary obligations and D&O insurance. But you absolutely need an *advisory board*, and the distinction matters less than you think.

An advisory board is a small group, three to five people is plenty, who meet with you quarterly to review the business, challenge your assumptions, and provide the kind of strategic perspective that's impossible to generate from inside the building. At least half of them should be independent: not family, not employees, not your golf buddies. People with relevant expertise who will tell you the truth even when the truth is uncomfortable.

Here's what your advisory board should be doing:

1. **Reviewing financial performance.** Not just the numbers, but the story behind them. Why did margins shrink? Is the revenue concentration in three clients a risk? Are we investing enough in the thing that'll matter in five years, or are we milking the thing that mattered five years ago?

2. **Pressure-testing strategic decisions.** Before you sign a $2 million lease or acquire a competitor or enter a new market, present the case to your board. Not for approval, for interrogation. Their job is to find the holes in your thinking before reality does.

3. **Monitoring succession planning.** If you've been reading this book in order, you know succession is a process, not an event. Your board should be reviewing that process regularly, assessing your successor's development, and holding you accountable to the timeline you set.

4. **Serving as a neutral zone.** When family disagreements threaten to spill into business decisions, the board becomes the adult in the room. This is especially critical during transitions, where emotions run high, and the temptation to make decisions based on guilt, loyalty, or resentment is almost irresistible.

How do you find good advisory board members? Start by looking at people who've already navigated what you're facing. Retired executives from your industry. Founders who've successfully transitioned their own businesses. Financial advisors who specialize in privately held companies. Your local university's business school might have experienced professors who serve on advisory boards as part of their community engagement. The point isn't pedigree, it's perspective. You want people who've seen around corners you haven't turned yet.

Compensation for advisory board members doesn't have to break the bank. A quarterly meeting fee of one to three thousand dollars per session, plus expenses, is standard for small to mid-sized businesses. Some members will do it for less, especially if they believe in what you're building. What matters is that you pay something, it signals that their time and input are valued, and it creates a professional expectation of preparation and candor.

Ring Three: Management Governance

This is the ring most founders ignore because they've been in the management governance structure their entire career. The founder decides. Period. That works until it doesn't, and the moment it stops working is usually the moment a second generation, a non-family executive, or a co-owner enters the picture.

Management governance defines the operating rules of the business itself: who has authority over what, how budgets get approved, what requires CEO sign-off versus what a department head can decide independently, and how performance is measured and rewarded. It's the organizational chart brought to life with actual decision rights.

Here's a practical exercise I recommend to every family business I work with: create a **Decision Rights Matrix**. Draw a grid. Across the top, list your key decision-makers by role, not by name. Down the side, list every significant category of decision the business faces, capital expenditures above a certain threshold, new hires, pricing changes, vendor contracts, client disputes, strategic partnerships. Then, for each combination, mark whether that role *decides, approves, is consulted,* or *is informed.* The DACI framework. It takes about two hours, and it eliminates about two years of passive-aggressive confusion.

The single most important row in that matrix is the one that defines what the CEO can do without board or ownership approval. Every family business needs a spending threshold, a number below which the CEO has full autonomy, and above which they need sign-off. Without that number, one of two things happens: either the CEO is paralyzed, running every purchase order past a committee, or the CEO is unchecked, making million-dollar commitments that the owners learn about after the fact. Neither is acceptable.

Governance Is a Gift, Not a Cage

I want to leave you with a reframe, because I know how this chapter might feel. If you're a founder, reading about advisory boards and decision matrices and family councils might feel like someone is building a cage around the thing you created with your bare hands. I get it.

But here's the truth: governance isn't a constraint on your business. It's a gift to everyone who will inherit it. Every ambiguity you clarify today is a conflict your children won't have to endure. Every decision-making process you formalize now is a power struggle your successors won't have to survive. You're not giving up control. You're *extending* it, past your tenure, past your retirement, past your lifetime.

The woman from the beginning of this chapter? She went home from that meeting and spent six months building a real governance structure. Family council. Advisory board. Decision rights matrix. The whole works. She told me later that the hardest part wasn't creating the structure. It was admitting she'd needed it all along. "I thought the fact that we all got along meant we didn't need rules," she said. "Now I understand that the rules are what will help us keep getting along."

She was right. And so are you, for reading this far.

You've got the governance architecture in place. The roles are defined, the decision-making process is clear, and you've got outside voices keeping everyone honest. Now comes the part where the blueprint meets reality, the messy, emotional, surprisingly long stretch of time between announcing the transition and actually completing it. This is where most handoffs fall apart, not because the plan was bad, but because nobody planned for what happens *during* it. In **Chapter 7: Managing the Transition Period**, we'll walk through how to communicate the change, how to handle the inevitable resistance from employees and clients, and how to navigate the strange no-man's-land where two leaders occupy the same building without the whole thing coming apart.

CHAPTER SEVEN

Managing the Transition Period

There's a phrase in aviation that every pilot learns early: *the most dangerous phase of flight is the transition.* Not cruising at altitude. Not sitting at the gate. It's the takeoff and landing, the moments when the aircraft is between two stable states, moving too fast to stop and too slow to climb. That's when the physics get tricky, when small errors compound, and when most accidents happen.

Your business transition works exactly the same way.

You've done the preparation. You've chosen your successor, separated family from finance, and built the governance structure. All of that was the pre-flight checklist. Now you're on the runway, engines spooling up, and the next twelve to twenty-four months will determine whether this thing takes off or slides into the grass.

This chapter is about that in-between. The period nobody writes about in the leadership books because it's unglamorous and uncomfortable and doesn't lend itself to tidy frameworks. It's the part where you're technically still the boss but functionally becoming a guest in your own company. It's the part where your successor is technically in charge, but everyone still looks past them to see if you're nodding.

Let's talk about how to survive it, and how to make sure the business does too.

The Two-Boss Problem

Here's the single biggest threat to your transition, and it has nothing to do with strategy, financials, or market conditions. It's this: for some period of time, your company will have two leaders. And organizations cannot function with two leaders any more than a car can function with two steering wheels.

I watched this play out at a mid-sized logistics company outside of Atlanta. The founder, call him Ray, had spent two years grooming his daughter, Elena, to take over. Smart, capable, well-prepared. They did everything right on paper. But when the transition began, Ray kept his corner office. He kept coming to the Monday leadership meetings. He kept walking on the warehouse floor. And every time a manager had a tough call to make, they'd walk past Elena's door and knock on Ray's. Not because Elena wasn't good. Because Ray was *there*, and twenty years of muscle memory told them that's where answers lived.

Elena lasted eight months before she called me and said, "I'm leading a company that won't let me lead."

The fix isn't complicated, but it requires something founders find almost physically painful: **you have to create a clear, visible, irreversible moment where authority transfers.** Not a gradual fade. Not a "co-leadership" arrangement. A line in the sand that everyone in the organization can see and understand.

This doesn't mean you disappear overnight. It means you define, in advance and in writing, what changes on Day One of the transition and what changes over the following months. A phased approach is fine. Ambiguity is not.

The Announcement: Getting It Right the First Time

How you announce the transition matters more than you think. Get it wrong, and you spend the next year cleaning up a narrative that formed in the first fifteen minutes.

Here's what most founders do: they send an email. A bland, HR-approved, three-paragraph email that says something like, "After much deliberation, I'm pleased to announce that effective January 1st, Jane Smith will assume the role of CEO." Everyone reads it, shrugs, and immediately starts speculating about what it really means. Was the founder pushed out? Is the company in trouble? Is Jane just keeping the seat warm?

Don't do that. Do this instead:

1. **Tell the inner circle first.** Before any company-wide announcement, sit down individually with your senior leaders, your key clients, and your most important partners. Tell them face-to-face. Explain the why, the timeline, and what it means for them specifically. These people are your amplifiers, if they're confident and informed, the rest of the organization will take its cues from them. If they're blindsided and anxious, that anxiety will cascade downward in hours.

2. **Make the announcement together.** You and your successor, side by side, in front of the whole team. Not a video. Not an email. In person, if at all possible. Your physical presence next to your successor sends a signal that no memo can match: this is my choice, I believe in this person, and we are aligned. If your company is too large or distributed for an all-hands meeting, do it via live video with a Q&A. The point is that people need to see your face and your successor's face at the same time.

3. **Name the elephant.** Everyone in the room will be thinking it: "Is this going to be okay?" Address it directly. Acknowledge that change is uncomfortable. Acknowledge that there will be a learning curve. Then explain, specifically, what's staying the same and what's changing. People can handle change; what they can't handle is uncertainty. The more concrete you are, the less room there is for the rumor mill.

4. **Let your successor speak.** This is not your farewell address. Give your successor at least half the stage time. Let them share their vision, their priorities, their personality. The team needs to start building a relationship with this person, and that can't happen if you're the one doing all the talking.

The First 100 Days: A Playbook for the In-Between

The concept of the first hundred days gets used so often in leadership transitions that it's become a cliché. But clichés become clichés because they're true. The first three months after the announcement will set the tone for the entire transition, and you need a deliberate plan for how both you and your successor will spend them.

For your successor, the first hundred days are about listening. Not launching initiatives, not reorganizing the chart, not proving they deserve the job. Listening. Meeting with every department head, every major client, every key vendor. Asking the same two questions over and over: "What's working that I should protect?" and "What's broken that nobody's been willing to fix?" The answers won't be surprising, your successor probably already knows most of them. But the act of asking signals humility, respect, and genuine curiosity. Those three qualities will buy more goodwill in a hundred days than a decade of strategic brilliance.

When Satya Nadella took over as CEO of Microsoft from Steve Ballmer, he didn't walk in with a sweeping reorganization plan. He spent his early months listening to employees, customers, and partners. He asked questions rather than issuing directives. The culture shift he's credited with engineering at Microsoft didn't start with a bold strategic pivot, it started with a leader who made people feel heard before he asked them to change.

For you, the outgoing leader, the first hundred days are about strategic withdrawal. This is the hardest part of the entire process, so let me give you a specific framework. Think of your involvement as a dimmer switch, not an on/off toggle. In Month One, you're at seventy-five percent brightness, present for major decisions, available for questions, still visible to the team. In Month Two, you drop to fifty, attending fewer meetings, deferring more questions to your successor, spending more time on transition logistics and less on operations. By Month Three, you're at twenty-five, available by phone for genuine emergencies, but physically absent from the day-to-day.

The dimmer switch only works if you commit to it publicly. Tell your team the plan. Tell them that when they come to you with a question in Month

Two, you're going to redirect them to your successor, not because you don't care, but because it's the only way the new relationship can form. If you don't name what you're doing, people will interpret your absence as disinterest rather than discipline.

Handling Resistance (Because It's Coming)

Not everyone will be happy about the transition. Some people will resist openly. Others will resist quietly, which is worse. Here's how resistance typically shows up, and what to do about each flavor.

The Loyalists. These are the people who are so personally devoted to you that they view any successor as an interloper. They'll say things like, "It won't be the same without you," which sounds like a compliment but functions as sabotage. They're signaling to the organization that the new leader is a downgrade. Your job is to redirect that loyalty, firmly and clearly. Pull them aside and say: "The best way to honor what we built together is to give the new leader the same commitment you gave me. That's what I'm asking you to do." Some will. Some won't. The ones who won't commit may need to leave, and you need to be okay with that.

The Opportunists. Every transition creates a power vacuum, and some people will try to exploit it. They'll go around the successor to you. They'll lobby for promotions they haven't earned. They'll try to renegotiate deals, territories, and reporting lines in the chaos. The antidote is the governance structure you built in Chapter 6, clear decision rights, clear authority, clear consequences. When someone tries an end-run, the response is simple: "That's a decision for the new CEO." Every single time.

The Flight Risks. Your best people, the ones with options, will quietly start taking calls from recruiters. Not because they want to leave, but because uncertainty makes talented people hedge their bets. Your successor needs to identify these people in the first thirty days and have individual conversations with each one. Not generic "we value you" conversations. Specific ones: "Here's where I see you in this organization over the next two years. Here's what I need from you. Here's what you can expect from me." Retention during transitions isn't about money. It's about vision. People stay when they can see a future worth staying for.

Clients, Vendors, and the Outside World

Internal transitions get all the attention, but the external transition is just as critical and frequently botched. Your clients and vendors have a relationship with you, and they need to form a new one with your successor. That doesn't happen through an introductory email.

Here's the approach that works → Co-manage every significant external relationship for at least sixty days. Bring your successor to client meetings, but don't run the meetings yourself. Introduce them, then sit back. Let the client see that your successor knows the account, knows the history, and knows the nuances. Your presence provides a safety net; their performance provides confidence. After sixty days, your successor goes alone.

For your most important relationships, the top five clients, the vendors you can't operate without, the banking relationships that keep the lights on, consider hosting a dinner or a small event where your successor can connect in a less formal setting. Business relationships run on trust, and trust forms faster over a meal than over a conference table. It sounds old-fashioned because it is. It works because people haven't changed.

One critical note: be honest with your external partners about the timeline. Don't pretend you'll be available forever. Tell them, "I'll be fully involved through June, available for questions through September, and then Maria will be your primary contact." Specificity builds confidence. Vagueness breeds anxiety.

When Things Go Wrong (And They Will)

I'd be lying if I told you transitions go smoothly. They don't. Something will break. A client will threaten to leave. A senior employee will resign. Your successor will make a decision you disagree with. The quarterly numbers will dip. It's going to happen, and how you respond in that moment will define whether the transition survives.

Here's the rule: **unless the building is literally on fire, do not intervene.** Your successor needs to handle it. If you swoop in and save the day, you've just told the entire organization that the new leader can't be trusted with hard problems. You've undermined months of work in a single afternoon. Instead, make yourself available privately. Call your successor that evening. Ask how they're thinking about it. Offer perspective if they want it. But let the decision, and the outcome, be theirs.

There is exactly one exception to this rule: if your successor is about to make a decision that could cause irreversible damage to the business, not a bad quarter, not a lost client, but an existential threat, you have a right and an obligation to speak up. But you do it privately, never in front of the team, and you frame it as counsel, not a command. The moment you issue a command, the transition is over. You're the boss again, and your successor is a figurehead.

The businesses that navigate transitions successfully share one trait: they accept the short-term performance dip as the cost of long-term continuity. Revenue might soften. Decision-making might slow down. Some things might get worse before they get better. That's normal. That's the turbulence during takeoff. It doesn't mean the plane is crashing.

The Finish Line Is Not What You Think

Here's something nobody tells you about the transition period: the hardest part isn't managing the business through it. It's managing *yourself.*

You're watching someone else make decisions about the thing you built. Some of those decisions will be better than yours would have been, and that will sting in a way you didn't expect. Some will be worse, and you'll have to bite your tongue until it bleeds. You'll feel irrelevant on Monday and indispensable on Tuesday and forgotten by Friday. You'll wonder if you made the right call. You'll wonder who you are without this company.

Those feelings are real, and they deserve more than a pep talk. They deserve their own chapter.

The operational playbook is in your hands. You know how to announce it, how to phase out, how to handle resistance, and how to keep clients from running for the exits. But there's a quieter, harder transition happening underneath all of that, the one inside your own head. In **Chapter 8: Letting Go, The Emotional Side of Exit**, we'll confront the identity crisis that nobody warns founders about, the grief that comes with leaving something you love, and how to walk away without losing the part of yourself you built along the way.

CHAPTER EIGHT

Letting Go, The Emotional Side of Exit

Three weeks after he handed the keys to his successor, a man I'll call Jim drove to his old office at 6:45 a.m., the same time he'd arrived every morning for twenty-six years. He sat in the parking lot for eleven minutes, engine running, watching the lights come on inside. Then he drove home, sat at his kitchen table, and cried.

Jim wasn't depressed, at least not clinically. He wasn't having second thoughts. The transition was going well. His successor was competent, and the team was adjusting. By every objective measure, Jim had executed a near-perfect exit.

He just didn't know who he was anymore.

If you've been reading this book in order, you've spent the last seven chapters building the machinery of a successful transition, the frameworks, the governance, the financial structures, the operational playbooks. All of that matters. But none of it prepares you for the thing that hits hardest: the *feeling* of leaving. The hollow Monday morning. The phone that stops ringing. The terrifying question you've been outrunning for decades: if I'm not the person who runs this company, who am I?

This is the chapter the business books don't write. Let's write it.

The Identity Trap

Here's what nobody tells you when you start a business: over the years, you don't just build a company. The company builds you. It becomes your identity, your social circle, your daily structure, your source of purpose, and, if you're being honest, your source of significance. When someone at a dinner party asks what you do, you don't say, "I enjoy woodworking, and I'm learning Italian." You say, "I run a manufacturing company." That's not a job description. That's a self-description.

Psychologists call this *identity fusion*, the point at which the boundary between self and role dissolves so completely that you can't tell where one ends and the other begins. It's extraordinarily common among founders and long-tenured leaders, and it's the reason so many of them sabotage their own exits. They're not clinging to the company because they think it can't survive without them. They're clinging to it because they're afraid *they* can't survive without it.

Phil Knight, in his memoir about building Nike, described the company as "my third child." That's not a throwaway line. When you've poured decades of your life into something, when you've missed recitals and anniversaries and vacations for it, when it's been the first thing you think about in the morning and the last thing you think about at night, walking away doesn't feel like retirement. It feels like an amputation.

So let's stop pretending this is easy, and let's stop pretending it's something you should just "get over." It's a legitimate loss, and it deserves to be treated like one.

The Five Stages of Founder Grief

I'm not being cute with this heading. The emotional arc of leaving a business you built tracks remarkably closely with the grief model, and recognizing where you are in it can keep you from making decisions you'll regret.

Denial sounds like: "I'm not really leaving. I'll still be involved. I'll be chairman emeritus, I'll come in on Tuesdays, I'll keep my email." This is you negotiating an exit that isn't really an exit. It feels rational. It isn't. It's a way to avoid the finality of the thing.

Anger sounds like: "They're already changing things. They moved the Monday meeting to Wednesday. They discontinued the product I launched in 2014. Don't they understand what I built?" Every change your successor makes will feel personal, even when it isn't. Especially when it isn't. Your anger isn't really about the meeting or the product. It's about the fact that the company is proving it can evolve without you, and that proof is excruciating.

Bargaining sounds like: "Maybe I should stay another year. Maybe I should keep the biggest client. Maybe I should take an advisory role with veto power." This is the stage where founders do the most damage, because the bargains always sound reasonable. They're not. They're your ego looking for a foothold in a building that no longer needs your load-bearing weight.

Sadness sounds like silence. It's Tuesday afternoon when you realize nobody needs you to approve anything. It's the industry conference where your successor is on the panel, and you're in the audience. It's the moment you walk past the building, and it looks exactly the same as it always did, and somehow that's the part that breaks your heart. This stage is real, it's healthy, and it's necessary. Don't skip it. Don't numb it. Sit in it long enough to learn what it's teaching you.

Acceptance doesn't sound like anything dramatic. It's the morning you wake up and realize you're thinking about what's next instead of what you left behind. It's the day your successor calls with a problem, and you feel genuine curiosity instead of the urge to take over. It's the first time someone asks what you do, and you give an answer that has nothing to do with the company. Acceptance doesn't mean you don't care anymore. It means the caring has changed shape.

What to Do With the Silence

The most disorienting part of leaving isn't the big moments. It's the quiet ones. For years, your calendar was a Tetris game of meetings, calls, crises, and decisions. Then, suddenly, it's Tuesday at 10 a.m., and nobody needs you for anything. The silence is deafening, and if you don't fill it deliberately, it will fill itself with regret, restlessness, and the overwhelming temptation to meddle.

Here's what I tell every exiting founder: you need to have something to go toward, not just something you're leaving behind. And you need to figure out what that is before your last day, not after.

1. **Rebuild your identity in advance.** Six months before your exit, start investing time in the parts of your life you've been neglecting. Relationships. Hobbies. Health. Community involvement. Not as a retirement checklist, but as a genuine exploration. What lights you up when the company isn't in the picture? You need to know this answer before the question becomes urgent.

2. **Find your tribe.** One of the loneliest aspects of exiting is losing your daily community. Your employees were your people, and now you see them at the occasional holiday party. You need a new tribe, other founders who've gone through this, mentors, peer groups, advisory networks. Organizations like Vistage, YPO, and EO have entire tracks for post-exit leaders. You'll be surprised how much it helps to sit in a room with people who understand exactly what you're feeling, because they've felt it too.

3. **Create a structure for your days.** This sounds almost embarrassingly simple, but it matters more than you'd think. Without the rhythm of work, days bleed into each other, and purposelessness creeps in fast. Build a weekly schedule that includes physical activity, social connection, intellectual stimulation, and at least one commitment that requires you to show up whether you feel like it or not. The structure won't feel natural at first. Give it ninety days.

4. **Consider a transition project.** Many founders find that going from full speed to full stop is too jarring. A transition project, mentoring another entrepreneur, joining a nonprofit board, consulting in your industry on a limited basis, writing, teaching, gives you a bridge between identities. It's not your company, and it shouldn't become your company.

But it gives your skills and experience a place to live while you figure out who you're becoming.

The Conversations Your Family Needs You to Have

While you're busy grieving the company, there are people in your house who've been waiting a long time for you to come home. And I don't mean physically, most founders have been physically present at dinner for years while being mentally checked out, running spreadsheets in their heads between bites of pasta.

Your spouse, your children, your close friends, they've experienced your exit too, and their experience is different from yours. Your spouse might be thrilled and terrified in equal measure: thrilled to finally have you present, terrified that you'll be miserable and make everyone around you miserable too. Your adult children might worry that your exit will rewrite the family financial picture. Your friends might not know how to relate to you outside the context of your professional identity.

Have the conversations. Tell your spouse what you're feeling, even when what you're feeling is confused and contradictory. Tell your kids that the transition is emotional for you, but that the plan is sound and the finances are secure. Tell your friends that you might be weird for a while and you'd appreciate their patience.

Vulnerability is not weakness. It's the same courage that built the company in the first place, the willingness to walk into uncertainty without knowing how it'll turn out. You've been doing that your entire career. You just didn't call it vulnerability. You called it *entrepreneurship.*

The Gift on the Other Side

I want to be honest with you: the first six months after exit are hard. For some people, they're the hardest six months of their lives. The identity work is real, the grief is real, and the disorientation is real.

But here's what the founders on the other side of it tell me, almost universally: they didn't just survive it. They discovered something they hadn't expected. Freedom. Not the Instagram version of freedom, not beaches and champagne. Real freedom. The freedom to wake up and choose what matters today without a P&L statement dictating the answer. The freedom to be present for the people they love without a phone vibrating in their pocket. The freedom to fail at something new without a hundred employees depending on the outcome.

Jim, the man who cried in his kitchen three weeks after leaving, called me eighteen months later. He'd started mentoring young entrepreneurs through a local incubator. He'd rebuilt his relationship with his wife, who told him it felt like falling in love with him again. He'd started fly fishing, badly, and he loved it. He said something I'll never forget: "I spent twenty-six years building something I was proud of. It took me a year to realize that wasn't the only thing I was capable of being proud of."

That's what's waiting for you. Not immediately. Not easily. But it's there.

You've confronted the hardest part, the part that lives in your chest, not on your balance sheet. But here's the question that ties everything in this book together: when the transition is complete, the emotions have settled, and the dust has cleared, what remains? What did all of this actually *mean?* In **Chapter 9: Legacy, Not Just Transfer**, we'll step back from the mechanics and the emotions and ask the biggest question of all, how to ensure that what you built doesn't just survive your departure, but carries forward the values, the vision, and the purpose that made it worth building in the first place.

CHAPTER NINE

Legacy, Not Just Transfer

There's a hardware store in Charlottesville, Virginia, that's been in the same family for four generations. The shelves are a little crooked. The floors creak in places the building inspector probably doesn't love. The prices are slightly higher than those at the big-box store three miles down the road. None of that matters. Every contractor within forty miles drives past that big-box store to shop here, because the kid behind the counter, who is now fifty-three years old and the great-grandson of the founder, knows their name, knows their project, and will stay twenty minutes past closing to help them find the right fastener.

That's not a business that was transferred. That's a business that was inherited in the deepest sense of the word. The product is lumber and screws. The legacy is something else entirely.

This chapter is about that *something else*, the invisible thing that separates a company that merely changes hands from one that carries forward across decades. We've spent eight chapters on the mechanics: how to plan the exit, value the business, choose a successor, build governance, manage the transition, and survive the emotional toll. All of it matters. But if you get all of that right and lose the soul of what you built, you haven't succeeded. You've just completed a transaction.

Legacy is what makes it more than that.

What Legacy Actually Is (And What It Isn't)

Let's start by clearing away the mythology. Legacy is not a bronze plaque in the lobby. It's not your name on the building or a framed photo of the founder in the conference room. Those are artifacts. They're nice, but they're wallpaper. Nobody changes how they treat a customer because there's a portrait hanging above the coffeemaker.

Legacy is the set of behaviors, values, and instincts that persist in an organization long after the person who planted them is gone. It's the reason one restaurant survives three ownership changes while the one next door loses its identity the moment the original chef leaves. It's the reason some companies still *feel* like themselves decades into the future, and others become unrecognizable within a year.

Think about Johnson & Johnson's response to the Tylenol crisis in 1982. When cyanide-laced capsules killed seven people in Chicago, the company pulled thirty-one million bottles from shelves at a cost of over a hundred million dollars, without hesitation, without a cost-benefit analysis, without lawyers telling them to wait. They did it because their credo, written by Robert Wood Johnson nearly forty years earlier, said that their first responsibility was to patients and consumers. That credo wasn't a marketing document. It was a *decision-making framework* embedded so deeply into the company's DNA that when the crisis came, the response was almost automatic. That's legacy. Not the credo on the wall. The behavior it produced under pressure.

Your legacy isn't what you say your company stands for. It's what your company does when nobody's watching, and the easy path leads in the other direction.

The Three Layers of Legacy

Legacy transmits across three layers, and most founders only think about one of them. If you want what you've built to outlast your tenure, you need to be intentional about all three.

Layer One: Values. These are the non-negotiable principles that define how the business operates, not aspirational poster slogans, but the real rules that govern decisions when they're hard. Do you prioritize long-term relationships over short-term revenue? Do you invest in your people even when the margins are tight? Do you tell clients the truth even when the truth costs you the deal? Whatever your actual values are, and I mean the ones you practice, not the ones on your website, they need to be articulated so clearly that your successor can apply them to situations you never imagined.

Here's a practical exercise: write down the five decisions you're most proud of in the history of your company. Not the biggest deals or the highest-revenue years, the decisions that defined *who you are* as a business. Then look at the pattern. What principle connects them? That pattern is your values, stripped of marketing language and revealed in action. Write those principles down and share them with your successor, not as rules to follow, but as a compass to navigate by.

Layer Two: Culture. Culture is values in motion. It's the way your values show up in daily behavior, how people talk to each other, how meetings are run, how mistakes are handled, how victories are celebrated, how newcomers are welcomed or excluded. Culture is famously hard to define and even harder to transfer because so much of it is unwritten.

Yvon Chouinard built a culture at Patagonia that survived not just leadership transitions but an entire ownership restructuring. When he transferred the company to a trust and a nonprofit in 2022, the fear was that the culture, the environmentalism, the employee empowerment, the willingness to tell customers *not* to buy a jacket they don't need, would erode without its founder's daily presence. It hasn't, because Chouinard didn't just practice the culture. He *codified* it. He wrote about it, talked about it, hired for it, fired over it, and built systems that reinforced it at every level of the organization. By the time he stepped away, the culture was self-sustaining. It didn't need Yvon anymore. It had become the company's operating system.

Your culture transfer checklist should look something like this:

1. **Document the rituals.** Every company has them, the way you celebrate

wins, the Friday afternoon tradition, the onboarding process that makes new hires feel like they belong. Write them down. They seem trivial until they're gone, and then everyone wonders why the place doesn't feel the same anymore.

2. **Identify the culture carriers.** In every organization, there are three or four people who *are* the culture. They embody it so naturally that new employees learn how to behave by watching them. Your successor needs to know who these people are and ensure they're protected, empowered, and retained. Losing a culture carrier during a transition can do more damage than losing a client.

3. **Tell the origin stories.** Every culture has founding myths, not myths in the fictional sense, but in the sense of stories that carry meaning. The time you stayed up all night to meet a client deadline. The time you turned down a lucrative deal because it conflicted with your principles. The time an employee made a mistake, and you responded with coaching instead of punishment. These stories teach values more effectively than any handbook. Share them with your successor. Better yet, create opportunities for them to be shared across the organization regularly.

Layer Three: Purpose. Values tell you how to act. Culture shows you how it looks. Purpose tells you *why it all matters.* This is the deepest layer, and it's the one that either survives generational transitions or doesn't.

Purpose isn't your mission statement. It's the answer to a question most companies never explicitly ask: beyond making money, why does this business exist? What problem does it solve that the world needs solving? What would be lost if it disappeared tomorrow?

For the hardware store in Charlottesville, the purpose was never about selling lumber. It was about being the place where the community's builders could get expert help from people who cared as much about the project as they did. Every generation of that family understood this instinctively, and every decision they made, from hiring to inventory to store hours, was filtered through it. That's why a four-generation hardware store can compete with a billion-dollar retailer. Purpose is the one advantage that can't be undercut by price.

Legacy Is a Conversation, Not a Monument

Here's a temptation you need to resist: the urge to freeze your legacy in amber. To write the values on the wall and declare them permanent. To insist that your successor maintain every tradition, every policy, every ritual exactly as you established it.

That isn't legacy. That's taxidermy.

A living legacy evolves. The core purpose stays constant, but its expression changes with the times. The hardware store's great-grandson didn't keep the business alive by running it exactly the way his great-grandfather did. He added an e-commerce platform. He started a YouTube channel with how-to videos. He redesigned the layout to be more accessible. He changed *everything* about how the business operated while changing *nothing* about why it existed. That's the distinction. Hold the purpose tight. Hold the methods loosely.

Your job as the outgoing leader isn't to dictate what the company will be forever. It's to make the purpose so clear, so deeply understood, and so genuinely compelling that your successor and their successor and the person after that will *want* to carry it forward, not because they have to, but because they believe in it as much as you do.

That requires trust. It requires the same kind of letting go we talked about in Chapter 8, but at a deeper level. You're not just letting go of the operations. You're letting go of the narrative. You're trusting that the story you started will be continued by someone who writes differently than you do but cares about the same ending.

Your Legacy Letter

I'm going to ask you to do something that might feel strange. I want you to write a letter. Not a memo, not a strategic plan, not a governance document. A letter, addressed to the person who will be running your company five years from now.

In this letter, tell them the story. Not the P&L story, the real story. Why you started this business. What you were scared of. What you sacrificed and what you gained. Tell them about the moment you almost quit and the moment you knew this was going to work. Tell them about the people who mattered most and the principles you refused to compromise on even when it cost you.

Then tell them what you hope for. Not specific targets or strategies, those will be obsolete by the time they read it. Tell them what you hope the business will feel like. What you hope customers will say about it. What you hope employees will feel when they walk through the door on a Monday morning.

This letter isn't a binding document. It's not a set of instructions. It's a conversation across time between the person who built something remarkable and the person who carries it forward. It's the most important thing you'll write about your business, and nobody will ever grade it. Write it for the person who needs to hear it. Write it honestly. Write it now, while the memories are still warm and the feelings are still real.

Then put it in a drawer. Your successor will find it when they need it. And they will need it.

What Remains

At the end of it all, after the succession plans and the governance structures, after the transition period and the emotional reckoning, after the contracts are signed and the titles have changed, what remains is the simplest thing in the world. Did you build something that matters? And did you leave it in the hands that will keep it mattering?

If you've read this book, you're the kind of person who cares enough to ask those questions. That alone puts you in rare company. Most people don't think about legacy until it's too late to shape it. You're thinking about it now, which means you still have time to be deliberate about the answer.

The business will change. It should change. But if you've done this work, the values work, the culture work, the purpose work, the essence of what you built will persist in ways you may never fully see. It will persist in the employee who stays late because they believe in the mission. In the client who refers a friend because they trust the company, not just the product. In the successor who faces a crisis and asks themselves, "What would the founder have done?", not to copy you, but to honor the standard you set.

That's your legacy. Not a plaque. Not a building. A standard that outlives you.

You've walked the entire path, from understanding why transitions fail to building the architecture that makes yours succeed, from choosing the right person to letting go of the identity you built along the way. There's only one thing left to do, and it's the most important thing of all: to start. In the **Conclusion: Your Next Chapter Starts Now**, we'll bring everything together into a single, actionable roadmap, and make sure the last page of this book is the first day of your transition.

Conclusion

Your Next Chapter Starts Now

You made it. Nine chapters, dozens of frameworks, and some conversations that probably hit closer to home than you expected. If you're still reading, it means you're serious, and that already puts you in a different category than most family business owners, who spend their entire careers meaning to get around to this.

But reading a book is not the same as building a plan. And I want to be direct with you about something: the gap between *knowing* what to do and *doing* it is where most exit plans go to die. Not because the information is bad, but because the first step is hard. Because it requires a phone call you don't want to make, or a conversation you've been avoiding, or an honest look at a number you're afraid to see.

So let's make this simple. Let's boil nine chapters down to what actually matters, look at the people who've done it, and give you a concrete plan for the next thirty days. Not the next three years. The next thirty days. Because if you can move in the next month, you'll move for the rest of the journey.

What You Now Know

Here's the book in nine sentences. Pin this somewhere you'll see it.

1. **Most transitions fail for human reasons, not business ones.** Silence, sentimentality, and procrastination kill more family businesses than bad markets ever will.
2. **Every exit plan stands on five pillars.** Valuation, succession, financial structure, operations, and family governance. If any one is missing, the whole thing is exposed.
3. **You need to know your number.** You cannot plan a transfer you haven't measured. Your tax strategy and your exit strategy are often in direct conflict, and the sooner you reconcile them, the more your business is worth.
4. **Your successor is not a younger version of you.** Choose based on the future, not the past. Test before you trust. And transfer the institutional knowledge that lives in your head before it walks out the door with you.
5. **Love is not a governance framework.** Separate family from finance with clear structures, market-rate compensation, formal agreements, and an outside voice in the room, so love never has to compete with money.
6. **Governance is a gift, not a cage.** Family councils, advisory boards, and decision rights matrices aren't bureaucracy. They're the systems that keep the business functioning when people disagree.
7. **The transition period is the danger zone.** Two leaders cannot steer the same ship. Create a visible, irreversible transfer of authority, dim your involvement on a clear schedule, and let your successor handle the turbulence.
8. **Letting go is grief, and grief is real.** The identity crisis isn't a weakness, it's the cost of having built something that mattered. Prepare for it before your last day, not after.
9. **Legacy is a standard, not a statue.** Hold the purpose tight and the methods loose. What you built will change. What it stands for doesn't

have to.

Proof It Works

Throughout this book, you met people who were exactly where you are, and who made it through. I want to bring them back one more time, because their endings matter as much as their beginnings.

Robert and Daniel nearly lost a $12 million plumbing supply company to the Founder's Trap. Robert couldn't stop calling the warehouse manager. Daniel was demoralized. Three key employees quit. But Robert did the hard work, defined his advisory role, stopped attending meetings he wasn't invited to, and gave Daniel the space to lead. Eighteen months later, Daniel was running the business. The warehouse manager came back. The company posted its best year in a decade.

Carol came to the exit planning process three years late and panicked when she saw the map. She had to compress a five-year plan into eighteen months. It was hard, and it was expensive. But she stopped waiting and started moving, got the valuation, resolved the succession question between her son and her operations manager, built the governance structure, and hit her retirement date. She now serves on the advisory board of the company her grandmother started, and her son calls her when he wants to, not when he has to.

Gary thought his HVAC distributorship was worth four times earnings until a real appraisal came back forty percent lower. Instead of being crushed, he got to work. Eighteen months of normalizing his financials, diversifying his customer base, and reducing owner dependency increased his valuation by thirty-one percent. Same business, better story, and a retirement he could actually afford.

Miguel and Sofia taught us the hardest lesson in the book: love is a terrible hiring criterion. But their story didn't end at Chapter 1. Miguel brought in a non-family COO to partner with Sofia, a hybrid structure that gave the business the operational discipline it needed while keeping Sofia's deep brand knowledge and customer relationships in play. Two years later, all five restaurant locations were profitable again.

Jim sat in his old parking lot three weeks after handing over the keys and cried. He didn't know who he was without the company. But Jim did the thing most founders won't, he sat with the grief instead of running back to the building. Eighteen months later, he was mentoring young entrepreneurs through a local incubator, had rebuilt his relationship with his wife, and had taken up fly fishing, badly. He told me something I'll never forget: "I spent twenty-six years building something I was proud of. It took me a year to realize that wasn't the only thing I was capable of being proud of."

David and Marcus nearly destroyed a fifteen-year brotherhood over a buyout conversation they'd been avoiding since day one. They ended up in litigation. They stopped speaking. Their mother had to choose which son to invite to Thanksgiving. But the story didn't end there. After eighteen months of legal battles that drained both of them financially and emotionally, they agreed to mediation. A family business consultant helped them do what they should have done years earlier, get a formal valuation, draft a real buy-sell agreement, and define a structured buyout timeline. David got his retirement. Marcus got the business. It took another year before Sunday dinners felt normal again, but they got there. The structures they finally built didn't just save the company. They saved the relationship.

These aren't extraordinary people. They're ordinary people who decided that the thing they built was worth protecting, and did the work to protect it. That's the only difference between a transition that succeeds and one that doesn't. Not talent. Not luck. Willingness.

Your Thirty-Day Launch Plan

You don't need to do everything at once. You need to do something this week. Here's your plan for the next thirty days, seven actions, each one tied directly to a chapter, each one designed to create enough momentum that stopping feels harder than continuing.

1. **Week One: Set your exit date and complete the Exit Readiness Scorecard** from Chapter 2. Pick a target year. Score yourself on the

five pillars. Circle the two lowest scores. Write them on a sticky note and put it on your bathroom mirror. This takes one hour, and it changes everything, because a plan without a deadline is a daydream.

2. **Week One: Call a business broker or M&A advisor** and ask for an initial conversation about what businesses like yours are selling for. You're not committing to anything. You're getting a number. That number will make every other decision in this process more grounded and more urgent.

3. **Week Two: Have the succession conversation.** Sit down with the person or people you're considering as successors and tell them, out loud, that you're beginning to plan your exit. You don't need to have all the answers. You need to break the silence. That conversation alone will shift the dynamic in ways you can't predict.

4. **Week Two: Run your own normalization.** Pull three years of financials. Identify every personal expense running through the business. Total the add-backs. Multiply by your industry multiple. The gap between your reported number and your normalized number is where the value is hiding.

5. **Week Three: Identify your governance gaps.** Do you have a buy-sell agreement? An operating agreement that reflects your current reality? A family employment policy? Write down which of these exist and which don't. Then call an attorney who actually specializes in closely held and family businesses, and schedule a meeting.

6. **Week Three: Start your relationship map.** Write down your ten most important business relationships, clients, vendors, bankers, partners. For each one, note what makes the relationship work and what your successor would need to know. This is the institutional knowledge transfer that saves two years of painful learning.

7. **Week Four: Schedule your Family Business Summit.** Pick a date within the next ninety days. Book a neutral location. Hire a facilitator. Invite every family member who has a stake in the business. This is where the real work begins, shared vision, structural gaps identified, accountability assigned. One day, off-site, no phones.

If you do these seven things in the next thirty days, you will have accomplished more toward your exit plan than most business owners accomplish in five years. That's not an exaggeration. Most owners are stuck in the *thinking-about-it* phase. You'll be in the *doing it* phase. The difference is everything.

Resources to Keep You Moving

You don't have to do this alone, and you shouldn't. Here are the professionals and organizations that will make the difference between a plan that sits in a drawer and one that actually gets executed.

Certified Valuation Analysts (CVA) and Accredited in Business Valuation (ABV) professionals provide defensible, IRS-ready business appraisals. The National Association of Certified Valuators and Analysts (NACVA) maintains a searchable directory at nacva.com. The American Institute of CPAs (AICPA) also credentials ABV professionals through its member directory.

Family Business Consultants specialize in the intersection of family dynamics and business strategy. The Family Firm Institute (FFI) at ffi.org is the leading global professional association, with a directory of credentialed advisors. The Family Business Consulting Group (FBCG) at thefbcg.com offers advisory services and a deep library of research.

Peer Networks for Business Owners provide the tribe you need during and after your transition. Vistage (vistage.com), the Young Presidents' Organization (ypo.org), and the Entrepreneurs' Organization (eonetwork.org) all offer structured peer groups and post-exit tracks for leaders navigating exactly what you're going through.

Estate and Business Transition Attorneys are essential for buy-sell agreements, trust structures, and ownership transfers. Look for attorneys who specialize in closely held or family businesses, not generalists. Your state bar association's lawyer referral service can help, and organizations like the American College of Trust and Estate Counsel (ACTEC) at actec.org maintain a fellowship of top practitioners.

Exit Planning Institute (EPI) at exit-planning-institute.org trains and certifies Certified Exit Planning Advisors (CEPA). Their advisor directory can connect you with professionals who specialize in building comprehensive exit plans across all five pillars.

Essential Reading. *Succession: Mastering the Make-or-Break Process of Leadership Transition* by Noel Tichy is the definitive work on leadership handoffs. *Keeping the Family Business Healthy* by John Ward remains the foundational text on multi-generational family enterprises. *Built to Last* by Jim Collins offers enduring lessons on building organizations that outlive their founders. And *Let Go to Grow* by Doug and Polly White is a practical guide to reducing owner dependency, the single most impactful value-building move most family businesses can make.

One Last Thing

I want to tell you something that nobody told me when I started working with family businesses, and that I wish someone had said out loud: this work is really worth it.

Not just financially, though the financial stakes are huge. Not just strategically, though the difference between a planned transition and a forced one is the difference between legacy and wreckage. It's worth it because of what it does to the people involved.

I've watched founders who spent decades avoiding hard conversations finally sit across from their children and say, "Here's what I built, here's what it's worth, and here's how we're going to make sure it survives." I've watched the relief wash over their faces. I've watched the next generation light up with a mixture of terror and pride that looks exactly like the expression their parents had when they started the company in the first place.

I've watched families who were drifting apart over unspoken resentments find their way back to each other, not because the resentments disappeared, but because the structures they built gave the resentments somewhere to go besides the dinner table.

And I've watched owners walk away from the thing they built, really walk away, cleanly, completely, and discover that they were more than their company. That the thing they were most afraid of losing turned out to be the thing that was keeping them from finding something they didn't know they needed.

That's what's on the other side of this work. Not just a transferred business. A family that's still whole. A legacy that's still breathing. And a founder who, for the first time in decades, has the freedom to find out what comes next.

You built something remarkable! Now go and make sure it lasts!

———————————————— ◆ ————————————————

The Family Business Exit Plan
How to Pass the Business to the Next Generation Without Losing It

About the Author

Mario A. Guzman has spent over two decades in the trenches of business growth, strategy, and leadership, from the factory floors of Caterpillar's global operations to the boardrooms of family-owned companies navigating their most consequential decisions. He is the President of **Growth Results Business Group**, a Miami-based consulting firm that helps business owners unlock revenue, optimize operations, and, through its dedicated Exit Preparation Consulting division, build the plans that allow family businesses to transition successfully from one generation to the next.

This book didn't come from theory. It came from sitting across the table from founders who had spent thirty years building something remarkable and had no idea how to hand it off without losing it. It came from watching brilliant businesses nearly collapse, not because of bad products or bad markets, but because nobody had addressed the human side of succession. And it came from a career spent learning, the hard way, that growth without a plan for what comes next is just building a bigger problem.

Background and Credentials

Mario holds three master's degrees: an **MBA in Business Administration and Management**, a **Master's in Entrepreneurship** from Western Carolina University, and a **Master's in Engineering Management** from the University of Dayton. He earned his Bachelor's in Mechanical Engineering from the Tecnológico de Monterrey, one of Latin America's premier institutions. He completed executive leadership programs at both **Cornell University** and **Bradley University**, and is a certified **Six Sigma Black Belt**, bringing data-driven rigor to every engagement he leads.

Before founding Growth Results Business Group, Mario spent over a decade at **Caterpillar Inc.**, where he held progressively senior roles spanning purchasing, Six Sigma project leadership, global supply chain management, and territory sales across Latin America. He led governmental merchandising programs that generated over $40 million annually, launched more than thirty new products to a network of thirty-two international dealers, and grew regional market share from thirty-five to forty-eight percent. His tenure at Caterpillar gave him a front-row education in market expansion, go-to-market strategies, and dealer network relationships.

He went on to serve as Vice President of Sales at Raycore Lights, where he implemented innovative marketing campaigns, and built the international dealer network from one market to seven markets across four continents. He also founded Groundbreaking Consulting, LLC, where he grew a consulting services portfolio to over $1.4 million in annual revenue and provided strategic advisory to small and medium family businesses, the work that planted the seeds for this book.

Services and Offerings

Through Growth Results Business Group, Mario and his team offer a range of consulting services designed to help business owners grow, optimize, and, when the time comes, exit on their own terms:

Exit Preparation Consulting for Family Businesses. The division was built specifically around the frameworks in this book. Whether you're five years from exit or five months, the team works with founders and their families to build comprehensive transition plans covering valuation, succession, governance, financial restructuring, and the emotional preparation that most advisors ignore. Every engagement is customized to the family's unique dynamics, because no two family businesses, or families, are alike.

Revenue Growth Strategy and Sales Operations. For businesses that aren't ready to exit yet but need to maximize value before they do, Mario's team designs and implements go-to-market strategies, sales infrastructure, and performance systems that drive measurable, sustainable growth.

Business Consulting and Advisory. From operational efficiency and process optimization to digital marketing and e-business development, Growth Results Business Group provides the strategic firepower that helps small and medium businesses compete at a higher level.

Workshops and Speaking. Mario is available for keynote presentations, half-day workshops, and multi-session programs on family business succession, exit planning, and building businesses that are transferable by design. He brings the same conversational, no-nonsense style you've experienced in this book. Contact his office for details.

Work With Mario and his Team!

If this book resonated with you, if you found yourself underlining sentences, recognizing your own family in the stories, or finally admitting that the plan you've been putting off needs to start now, the next step is a conversation.

No pitch. No pressure. Just an honest assessment of where you stand and what it would take to get where you want to go.

You can connect with me on:

🌐 https://www.grbg.llc